BEATLES

TRIVIA BOOK

▲▼▲▼▲▼▲▼▲▼▲▼▲▼▲▼▲▼▲▼▲▼▲▼▲▼▲▼▲▼▲▼▲▼▲▼▲▼

250 QUESTIONS ABOUT THE FAB FOUR

INCLUDING THE SOLO CAREERS OF PAUL McCARTNEY, JOHN LENNON, GEORGE HARRISON & RINGO STARR

☆ BY STEVEN MILLER ☆

VOLUME 3

Copyright © 2018 by Western Reserve Books

Library of Congress Cataloging-in-Publication Data
Miller, Steven
ISBN: 9781729318713

> Beatles Trivia Book: Including the Solo Careers of
> Paul McCartney, John Lennon, George Harrison &
> Ringo Starr, Volume 3
> 1. Rock music
> I. Title

QUESTION #1: Who was the guest guitarist on the Beatles song, "While My Guitar Gently Weeps"?
A. Keith Richard
B. Billy Preston
C. Jeff Beck
D. Eric Clapton

QUESTION #2: In the mid-1990s, two unfinished John Lennon tracks were completed by the surviving members of the Beatles, "Free As A Bird" and what other song?
A. "Brownbird"
B. "Darling Don't"
C. "Real Love"
D. "Darling Love"

QUESTION #3: After the Beatles disbanded, who was the first member of the group to perform at the Cavern Club in Liverpool?
A. John Lennon
B. Paul McCartney
C. George Harrison
D. Ringo Starr

QUESTION #4: In 1976, which Beatle purchased the publishing rights to Buddy Holly's song catalog?
A. John Lennon
B. Paul McCartney
C. George Harrison
D. Ringo Starr

ANSWER #1: D. Eric Clapton was invited to play on the session by George Harrison.
ANSWER #2: C. "Real Love"
ANSWER #3: B. Paul McCartney performed a much-publicized concert at the rebuilt Cavern Club in 1999.
ANSWER #4: B. Paul McCartney

QUESTION #5: Who came up with idea for the Beatles to bow in unison after every song?
A. Brian Epstein
B. Astrid Kirchherr
C. Stuart Sutcliffe
D. Pete Best

QUESTION #6: Which Beatle directed the 1972 film documentary about Marc Bolan, "Born To Boogie"?
A. John Lennon
B. Paul McCartney
C. George Harrison
D. Ringo Starr

QUESTION #7: How many U.S. singles were issued from "Sgt. Pepper's Lonely Hearts Club Band" at the time of the album's release?
A. 0
B. 1
C. 2
D. 3

QUESTION #8: Which Beatles song was the first top-40 hit to feature a fade-in intro?
A. "Strawberry Fields Forever"
B. "Eight Days A Week"
C. "Norwegian Wood"
D. "All My Loving"

_____

ANSWER #5: A. Brian Epstein
ANSWER #6: D. Ringo Starr
ANSWER #7: A. 0. No singles were issued from the album at the time of its release. In the late-1970s, the title track was issued as a single.
ANSWER #8: B. "Eight Days A Week"

QUESTION #9: Which former Beatles recording engineer scored a solo top-40 hit in the 1970s?
A. Allan Rouse
B. Bob Ezrin
C. George Martin
D. Hurricane Smith

QUESTION #10: Which of these Beatles songs fueled the rumors that "Paul was dead"?
A. "A Day In The Life"
B. "Let It Be"
C. "Across The Universe"
D. "Strawberry Fields Forever"

QUESTION #11: Which Beatles song was written by Paul McCartney to console Julian Lennon during the divorce of his parents?
A. "Help!"
B. "You've Got To Hide Your Love Away"
C. "All My Loving"
D. "Hey Jude"

QUESTION #12: Which John Lennon single was issued as by John Lennon with the Plastic Ono Nuclear Band?
A. "Give Peace A Chance"
B. "Mind Games"
C. "Imagine"
D. "Whatever Gets You Thru The Night"

ANSWER #9: D. Hurricane Smith scored a top-40 hit in 1972 with "Oh Babe, What Would You Say?"
ANSWER #10: D. "Strawberry Fields Forever" included lyrics that were often misheard as "I buried Paul."
ANSWER #11: D. "Hey Jude"
ANSWER #12: D. "Whatever Gets You Thru The Night"

QUESTION #13: Which rock band was named after a Beatles song?
A. Argent
B. Badfinger
C. Love
D. Matchbox Twenty

QUESTION #14: What was the name of the group led by Paul McCartney's brother, Mike McGear, that reached the British top-10 in 1974 with an album produced by Paul McCartney?
A. Scaffold
B. Slade
C. Brian & Michael
D. Liverpool Express

QUESTION #15: Who was the first Beatle to appear on the television program, "The Simpsons"?
A. John Lennon
B. Paul McCartney
C. George Harrison
D. Ringo Starr

QUESTION #16: The back cover of which album by Paul McCartney & Wings featured a message to Stevie Wonder written in braille?
A. "Band On The Run"
B. "Red Rose Speedway"
C. "Ram"
D. "Venus And Mars"

ANSWER #13: B. Badfinger. "Bad Finger Boogie" was the original, working title of the Beatles song, "With A Little Help From My Friends."
ANSWER #14: A. Scaffold. Mike McGear's real name is Peter Michael McCartney.
ANSWER #15: D. Ringo Starr
ANSWER #16: B. "Red Rose Speedway." The message read: "We love ya baby."

QUESTION #17: According to Paul McCartney, his solo hit "Jet" was written about what?
A. His dog
B. His cat
C. His first car
D. His first bicycle

QUESTION #18: None of the four Beatles played any instruments on which of these songs?
A. "She's A Woman"
B. "I Want You (She's So Heavy)"
C. "Eleanor Rigby"
D. "I Am The Walrus"

QUESTION #19: What was the final song performed by the Beatles at their last-ever paid concert at San Francisco's Candlestick Park on August 29, 1966?
A. "Long Tall Sally"
B. "Blueberry Hill"
C. "Twist And Shout"
D. "Shout"

QUESTION #20: The lead guitarist on the Elton John hit "Lucy In The Sky With Diamonds" was listed as Dr. Winston O'Boogie, who in real life was which Beatle?
A. John Lennon
B. Paul McCartney
C. George Harrison
D. Ringo Starr

ANSWER #17: A. His dog
ANSWER #18: C. "Eleanor Rigby"
ANSWER #19: A. "Long Tall Sally"
ANSWER #20: A. John Lennon

QUESTION #21: In 1972, which Beatle hosted *The Mike Douglas Show* for an entire week?
A. John Lennon
B. Paul McCartney
C. George Harrison
D. Ringo Starr

❖ ❖ ❖

QUESTION #22: The lyrics of the Beatles song "Being For The Benefit Of Mr. Kite" were based on what?
A. A newspaper advertisement
B. A children's novel
C. A crime magazine
D. A circus poster

❖ ❖ ❖

QUESTION #23: In 1974, which former Beatle started his own label, Dark Horse Records?
A. John Lennon
B. Paul McCartney
C. George Harrison
D. Ringo Starr

❖ ❖ ❖

QUESTION #24: Which Beatles single was issued as by "The Beatles and Billy Preston"?
A. "Come Together"
B. "Let It Be"
C. "Get Back"
D. "All You Need Is Love"

❖ ❖ ❖

QUESTION #25: On July 5, 1968, which Beatle sold his famous, psychedelic Rolls Royce?
A. John Lennon
B. Paul McCartney
C. George Ringo
D. Ringo Starr

ANSWER #21: A. John Lennon and Yoko Ono hosted the program in February 1972.
ANSWER #22: D. A circus poster
ANSWER #23: C. George Harrison
ANSWER #24: C. "Get Back" was released in 1969. The single's B-side was "Don't Let Me Down."
ANSWER #25: A. John Lennon

QUESTION #26: Which of the following is NOT the nickname of a Beatles album?
A. The White Album
B. The Blue Album
C. The Red Album
D. The Yellow Album

❖ ❖ ❖

QUESTION #27: In 1979, which Beatle published his autobiography, "I Me Mine"?
A. John Lennon
B. Paul McCartney
C. George Harrison
D. Ringo Starr

❖ ❖ ❖

QUESTION #28: In 1979, the wife of which Beatle issued a single as by Suzy & The Red Stripes?
A. John Lennon
B. Paul McCartney
C. George Harrison
D. Ringo Starr

❖ ❖ ❖

QUESTION #29: Which hit song by Paul McCartney & Wings featured bagpipes?
A. "Mull Of Kintyre"
B. "Helen Wheels"
C. "Let 'Em In"
D. "Maybe I'm Amazed"

❖ ❖ ❖

QUESTION #30: At his Super Bowl halftime performance in 2005, Paul McCartney sang three Beatles songs and which solo hit?
A. "Live And Let Die"
B. "Band On The Run"
C. "Silly Love Songs"
D. "Maybe I'm Amazed"

ANSWER #26: D. The Yellow Album
ANSWER #27: C. George Harrison
ANSWER #28: B. Paul McCartney also produced his wife's single.
ANSWER #29: A. "Mull Of Kintyre"
ANSWER #30: A. "Live And Let Die"

QUESTION #31: The Concert for Bangladesh was staged in which city?
A. Tokyo
B. Rome
C. Los Angeles
D. New York

❖ ❖ ❖

QUESTION #32: Which of these Beatles songs featured the sound of an airplane?
A. "Being For The Benefit Of Mr. Kite"
B. "I Want You (She's So Heavy)"
C. "Back In The U.S.S.R."
D. "I Am The Walrus"

❖ ❖ ❖

QUESTION #33: In a tribute to John Lennon, Roxy Music topped the British charts in 1981 with a remake of which Lennon song?
A. "Whatever Gets You Through The Night"
B. "#9 Dream"
C. "Imagine"
D. "Jealous Guy"

❖ ❖ ❖

QUESTION #34: Which 45rpm single by Paul McCartney featured the same song on both sides of the record?
A. "Jet"
B. "Live And Let Die"
C. "Helen Wheels"
D. "Coming Up"

❖ ❖ ❖

QUESTION #35: The album "Band On The Run" by Paul McCartney & Wings was recorded in which African country?
A. Sudan
B. Morocco
C. Nigeria
D. Liberia

ANSWER #31: D. New York. There were actually two concerts staged at Madison Square Garden on August 1, 1971.
ANSWER #32: C. "Back In The U.S.S.R."
ANSWER #33: D. "Jealous Guy"
ANSWER #34: D. "Coming Up"
ANSWER #35: C. Nigeria

QUESTION #36: What was the original title of the Beatles film, "Help!"?
A. "Eight Arms to Hold You"
B. "Beatlemania"
C. "Yes It Is"
D. "Ticket To Ride"

QUESTION #37: What year did Ringo Starr publically announce that he would no longer sign autographs?
A. 1978
B. 1988
C. 1998
D. 2008

QUESTION #38: In 1964, the Beatles were asked at a press conference, "Are you going to get a haircut at all while you're here?" Which Beatle responded, "I had one yesterday"?
A. John Lennon
B. Paul McCartney
C. George Harrison
D. Ringo Starr

QUESTION #39: Who came up with the name of the Beatles business venture, Apple Corps?
A. Brian Epstein
B. Allen Klein
C. Paul McCartney
D. John Lennon

ANSWER #36: D. "Ticket To Ride." Some pressings of the single "Ticket To Ride" state that the song is from the forthcoming film, "Eight Arms To Hold You."
ANSWER #37: D. 2008
ANSWER #38: C. George Harrison
ANSWER #39: C. Paul McCartney

QUESTION #40: Which Beatles track did John Lennon describe as his "first psychedelic song"?
A. "Dear Prudence"
B. "Day Tripper"
C. "Tomorrow Never Knows"
D. "Being For The Benefit Of Mr. Kite"

❖ ❖ ❖

QUESTION #41: Paul McCartney released his debut solo album "McCartney" in 1970. When did he release the album, "McCartney II"?
A. 1975
B. 1980
C. 1985
D. 1990

❖ ❖ ❖

QUESTION #42: What was the Beatles' first hit in Britain?
A. "Love Me Do"
B. "P.S. I Love You"
C. "Please Please Me"
D. "I Want To Hold Your Hand"

❖ ❖ ❖

QUESTION #43: How many Americans watched the first performance by the Beatles on "The Ed Sullivan Show" in 1964?
A. 53 million
B. 63 million
C. 73 million
D. 83 million

❖ ❖ ❖

QUESTION #44: After signing the Beatles, Brian Epstein launched a management company called NEMS Enterprises. What does NEMS stand for?
A. New England Music Shoppe
B. North End Music Stores
C. North Etting Matching Silverware
D. Neil Epstein's Music Shop

ANSWER #40: C. "Tomorrow Never Knows"
ANSWER #41: B. 1980
ANSWER #42: A. "Love Me Do"
ANSWER #43: C. 73 million
ANSWER #44: B. North End Music Stores

QUESTION #45: Which of these Beatles songs did NOT feature Ringo Starr on lead vocals?
A. "Yellow Submarine"
B. "Act Naturally"
C. "With A Little Help From My Friends"
D. "All My Loving"

QUESTION #46: Which of these Beatles songs did NOT feature George Harrison on lead vocals?
A. "Something"
B. "Here Comes The Sun"
C. "If I Fell"
D. "While My Guitar Gently Weeps"

QUESTION #47: Which Beatles song had a working title of "Scrambled Eggs"?
A. "A Day In The Life"
B. "Hey Jude"
C. "Yesterday"
D. "Let It Be"

QUESTION #48: By 1962, the Beatles were playing for capacity crowds at the Cavern Club in Liverpool. How many people could the club hold?
A. 300
B. 500
C. 700
D. 900

ANSWER #45: D. "All My Loving"
ANSWER #46: C. "If I Fell"
ANSWER #47: C. "Yesterday"
ANSWER #48: D. 900 fans showed up for the lunchtime performances.

QUESTION #49: At a news conference in 1964, who did George Harrison jokingly refer to as "the Fifth Beatle"?
A. Murray the K
B. Brian Epstein
C. Tony Sheridan
D. Derek Taylor

❖ ❖ ❖

QUESTION #50: Vee-Jay Records issued the compilation album, "The Beatles and Frank Ifield On Stage." Although Ifield was a major star in Britain, what was his only U.S. top-40 hit?
A. "Lovesick Blues"
B. "I Remember You"
C. "Young Love"
D. "Telstar"

❖ ❖ ❖

QUESTION #51: The Beatles scored their biggest-ever hit on the U.S. country charts when Rosanne Cash recorded which of the group's songs in 1989?
A. "Yesterday"
B. "Eleanor Rigby"
C. "I Feel Fine"
D. "I Don't Want To Spoil The Party"

❖ ❖ ❖

QUESTION #52: Which Beatle provided the whispering background vocal on Donovan's 1966 hit, "Mellow Yellow"?
A. John Lennon
B. Paul McCartney
C. George Harrison
D. Ringo Starr

ANSWER #49: A. Murray the K was the nickname of popular New York City deejay Murray Kaufman. He earned "the Fifth Beatle" designation after befriending the Beatles during their first trip to the U.S. in February 1964.
ANSWER #50: B. "I Remember You"
ANSWER #51: D. "I Don't Want To Spoil The Party"
ANSWER #52: B. Paul McCartney

QUESTION #53: In 1965, Brian Epstein hosted a musical segment that aired on which American television show?
A. Hullabaloo
B. Shindig!
C. Where The Action Is
D. The Dean Martin Show

❖ ❖ ❖

QUESTION #54: Who coined the term, "Fab Four"?
A. Stuart Sutcliffe
B. Tony Burrows
C. Phil Spector
D. Brian Epstein

❖ ❖ ❖

QUESTION #55: What was the Beatles' first number-one single in the U.S.?
A. "She Loves You"
B. "Hey Jude"
C. "Let It Be"
D. "I Want To Hold Your Hand"

❖ ❖ ❖

QUESTION #56: Who was the oldest member of the Beatles?
A. John Lennon
B. Paul McCartney
C. George Harrison
D. Ringo Starr

❖ ❖ ❖

QUESTION #57: The Gideon's Bible is mentioned in which Beatles song?
A. "Penny Lane"
B. "Matchbox"
C. "Rocky Racoon"
D. "Eleanor Rigby"

ANSWER #53: A. Hullabaloo
ANSWER #54: B. Tony Burrows was the Beatles' press officer.
ANSWER #55: D. "I Want To Hold Your Hand"
ANSWER #56: D. Ringo Starr was born on July 7, 1940, and is the oldest. The youngest was George Harrison who was born on February 25, 1943.
ANSWER #57: C. "Rocky Racoon"

QUESTION #58: In which film is Ringo Starr's character nearly sacrificed by members of an Eastern cult?
A. "Magical Mystery Tour"
B. "Yellow Submarine"
C. "Help!"
D. "A Hard Day's Night"

QUESTION #59: When a judge ruled George Harrison's "My Sweet Lord" was similar to the Chiffons's "He's So Fine," how much was Harrison ordered to pay?
A. $187,000
B. $387,000
C. $587,000
D. $787,000

QUESTION #60: George Harrison and the rest of the Traveling Wilburys recorded nearly all of the tracks for their first album at whose home?
A. David A. Stewart
B. Mick Fleetwood
C. Tom Petty
D. Jeff Lynne

QUESTION #61: Paul McCartney signed singer Mary Hopkin to Apple Records and produced her debut hit, "Those Were The Days." Who had recommended Hopkin to McCartney?
A. George Martin
B. Richard Burton
C. Eric Burdon
D. Twiggy

ANSWER #58: C. "Help!"
ANSWER #59: C. $587,000
ANSWER #60: A. David A. Stewart
ANSWER #61: D. Twiggy, the British fashion model, had spotted Mary Hopkin on a British talent show.

QUESTION #62: When the Beatles recorded several tracks with singer Tony Sheridan, they were originally billed on the record under what name?
A. The Silver Beatles
B. The Hamburg Beatles
C. The Beat Brothers
D. The Sheridans

❖ ❖ ❖

QUESTION #63: During their 1964 U.S. tour, what was the most the Beatles were paid for a single concert?
A. $150,000
B. $300,000
C. $500,000
D. $650,000

❖ ❖ ❖

QUESTION #64: Which Beatle was pictured sitting inside a trunk on the front cover of the album, "Yesterday And Today"?
A. John Lennon
B. Paul McCartney
C. George Harrison
D. Ringo Starr

❖ ❖ ❖

QUESTION #65: Which Beatle married a "Bond Girl"?
A. John Lennon
B. Paul McCartney
C. George Harrison
D. Ringo Starr

❖ ❖ ❖

QUESTION #66: In 1961, John Lennon wrote articles for which publication?
A. Mersey Beat
B. New Musical Express
C. Melody Maker
D. The Daily Mail

ANSWER #62: C. The Beat Brothers
ANSWER #63: A. $150,000
ANSWER #64: B. Paul McCartney
ANSWER #65: D. Ringo Starr married actress Barbara Bach in 1981. She had starred in the James Bond film, *The Spy Who Loved Me*.
ANSWER #66: A. Mersey Beat

QUESTION #67: Keyboard player Gary Brooker of Procol Harum was previously a member of which band managed by Brian Epstein?
A. The Rustiks
B. The Paramounts
C. The Remo Four
D. Billy J. Kramer & The Dakotas

❖ ❖ ❖

QUESTION #68: Which future Beatle suffered a life-threatening bout of tuberculous in 1955?
A. John Lennon
B. Paul McCartney
C. George Harrison
D. Ringo Starr

❖ ❖ ❖

QUESTION #69: Which Beatles song appeared in a commercial for Target stores in 2008?
A. "Ticket To Ride"
B. "Get Back"
C. "Come Together"
D. "Hello Goodbye"

❖ ❖ ❖

QUESTION #70: Who was the first member of the Beatles to get married?
A. John Lennon
B. Paul McCartney
C. George Harrison
D. Ringo Starr

❖ ❖ ❖

QUESTION #71: Which Beatles song was named after a street in Los Angeles?
A. "Penny Lane"
B. "Blue Jay Way"
C. "Strawberry Fields Forever"
D. "The Long And Winding Road"

ANSWER #67: B. The Paramounts
ANSWER #68: D. Ringo Starr
ANSWER #69: D. "Hello Goodbye"
ANSWER #70: A. John Lennon married Cynthia Powell on August 23, 1962. They would divorce six years later.
ANSWER #71: B. "Blue Jay Way"

QUESTION #72: What was the first Beatles record played on "American Bandstand"?
A. "I Want To Hold Your Hand"
B. "Love Me Do"
C. "Please Please Me"
D. "She Loves You"

QUESTION #73: Which member of the Beatles wore a white suit on the cover of "Abbey Road"?
A. John Lennon
B. Paul McCartney
C. George Harrison
D. Ringo Starr

QUESTION #74: In 1969, Aretha Franklin scored a pop hit with a remake of which Beatles song?
A. "Something"
B. "Yesterday"
C. "Let It Be"
D. "Eleanor Rigby"

QUESTION #75: A musical performance by which group was filmed for "Magical Mystery Tour," but was cut from the movie?
A. The Yardbirds
B. Cream
C. Traffic
D. The Animals

QUESTION #76: Which 1960s pop group was managed by Brian Epstein and named by John Lennon?
A. Gerry & The Pacemakers
B. Billy J. Kramer and the Dakotas
C. The Remo Four
D. The Cyrkle

ANSWER #72: D. "She Loves You." It aired during the Rate-A-Record segment in late-1963, and the song received a score of 73.
ANSWER #73: A. John Lennon
ANSWER #74: D. "Eleanor Rigby"
ANSWER #75: C. Traffic
ANSWER #76: D. The Cyrkle

QUESTION #77: Which Beatles movie was filmed in black and white?

A. "Yellow Submarine"
B. "Help"
C. "Magical Mystery Tour"
D. "A Hard Day's Night"

❖ ❖ ❖

QUESTION #78: Published in 1964, the book "In His Own Write" was written by which Beatle?

A. John Lennon
B. Paul McCartney
C. George Harrison
D. Ringo Starr

❖ ❖ ❖

QUESTION #79: Which Beatles song was used as the title of a Beatles-related movie, which starred Jim Stirges and Evan Rachel Wood?

A. "Across The Universe"
B. "She Loves You"
C. "Can't Buy Me Love"
D. "She's A Woman"

❖ ❖ ❖

QUESTION #80: Who was removed from the planned cover of "Sgt. Pepper's Lonely Hearts Club Band" after demanding a payment for the use of his image?

A. Jerry Lewis
B. Sam Phillips
C. Woody Guthrie
D. Leo Gorcey

ANSWER #77: D. "A Hard Day's Night." United Artists began planning the film in 1963, which was before the Beatles were known in the U.S. But despite the group's growing popularity, the studio refused to film the movie in color.

ANSWER #78: A. John Lennon

ANSWER #79: A. "Across The Universe"

ANSWER #80: D. Leo Gorcey. Although Gorcey was not on the cover, his *Bowery Boys* co-star, Huntz Hall, was pictured.

QUESTION #81: The 1964 Beatles tribute record, "Ringo, I Love You," was recorded by Bonnie Jo Mason and produced by Phil Spector. Bonnie Jo Mason is better known by what other name?
A. Olivia Newton-John
B. Ronnie Spector
C. Mama Cass
D. Cher

QUESTION #82: In 1964, who appeared as a guest contestant on the CBS television show, "I've Got A Secret"?
A. Ringo Starr
B. Pete Best
C. Stuart Sutcliffe
D. Brian Epstein

QUESTION #83: In 1969, newlyweds John Lennon and Yoko Ono spent their honeymoon with members of the press in a hotel room in what city?
A. Amsterdam
B. London
C. Montreal
D. Paris

QUESTION #84: What was the very first song performed by the Beatles on "The Ed Sullivan Show"?
A. "She Loves You"
B. "I Want To Hold Your Hand"
C. "Please Please Me"
D. "All My Loving"

ANSWER #81: D. Cher. Her future husband, Sonny Bono, also worked on the record.
ANSWER #82: B. Pete Best
ANSWER #83: A. Amsterdam
ANSWER #84: D. "All My Loving"

QUESTION #85: Who was the only Beatle to perform at the legendary Apollo Theater in New York City?
A. John Lennon
B. Paul McCartney
C. George Harrison
D. Ringo Starr

❖ ❖ ❖

QUESTION #86: Which Beatle wrote and produced Badfinger's 1970 hit, "Come And Get It"?
A. John Lennon
B. Paul McCartney
C. George Harrison
D. Ringo Starr

❖ ❖ ❖

QUESTION #87: Which Beatles song was originally a hit in 1927 for Ben Bernie and his Orchestra?
A. "Devil In Her Heart"
B. "Maggie Mae"
C. "Ain't She Sweet"
D. "Mr. Moonlight"

❖ ❖ ❖

QUESTION #88: After the breakup of the Beatles, who was the first member of the group to launch a solo U.S. tour?
A. John Lennon
B. Paul McCartney
C. George Harrison
D. Ringo Starr

❖ ❖ ❖

QUESTION #89: Which Beatle scored a top-40 hit in the early-1970s with a rock version of a nursery rhyme?
A. John Lennon
B. Paul McCartney
C. George Harrison
D. Ringo Starr

ANSWER #85: B. Paul McCartney
ANSWER #86: B. Paul McCartney. The song was featured in the Peter Sellers film, "The Magic Christian."
ANSWER #87: C. "Ain't She Sweet"
ANSWER #88: C. George Harrison
ANSWER #89: B. Paul McCartney and Wings scored a top-40 hit in 1972 with "Mary Had A Little Lamb."

QUESTION #90: Who was the first Beatle to score a top-10 solo single and album in the U.S.?

A. John Lennon
B. Paul McCartney
C. George Harrison
D. Ringo Starr

❖ ❖ ❖

QUESTION #91: What year did Paul McCartney perform at the Grammy Awards for the first time?

A. 1976
B. 1986
C. 1996
D. 2006

❖ ❖ ❖

QUESTION #92: Which member of the Beatles scored a minor top-40 U.S. hit in the mid-1970s with the holiday single, "Ding Dong, Ding Dong"?

A. John Lennon
B. Paul McCartney
C. George Harrison
D. Ringo Starr

❖ ❖ ❖

QUESTION #93: In 1963, "She Loves You" by the Beatles set the record for the best-selling single in Britain. In the 1970s, which single broke that record?

A. "Feelings" by Morris Albert
B. "Let It Be" by the Beatles
C. "Saturday Night" by the Bay City Rollers
D. "Mull Of Kintyre" by Paul McCartney & Wings

ANSWER #90: A. John Lennon
ANSWER #91: D. 2006
ANSWER #92: C. George Harrison
ANSWER #93: D. "Mull Of Kintyre" by Paul McCartney & Wings. The single was only a minor hit in the U.S.

QUESTION #94: The Ringo Starr song, "Back Off Boogaloo," was allegedly written about whom?

A. John Lennon

B. Paul McCartney

C. Eric Clapton

D. Joe Cocker

❖ ❖ ❖

QUESTION #95: After the Beatles disbanded, who was the first solo Beatle to record an album produced by George Martin?

A. John Lennon

B. Paul McCartney

C. George Harrison

D. Ringo Starr

❖ ❖ ❖

QUESTION #96: Which Beatle appeared in the music video for the song, "They Don't Know" by Tracey Ullman?

A. John Lennon

B. Paul McCartney

C. George Harrison

D. Ringo Starr

❖ ❖ ❖

QUESTION #97: Which Beatle played the guitar on Belinda Carlisle's top-40 hit "Leave A Light On"?

A. John Lennon

B. George Harrison

C. Ringo Starr

D. Paul McCartney

❖ ❖ ❖

QUESTION #98: What was the only song on the album "Let It Be... Naked" that did not appear on the original "Let It Be" release?

A. "Dig A Pony"

B. "For You Blue"

C. "I Me Mine"

D. "Don't Let Me Down"

ANSWER #94: B. Paul McCartney

ANSWER #95: D. Ringo Starr

ANSWER #96: B. Paul McCartney

ANSWER #97: B. George Harrison

ANSWER #98: D. "Don't Let Me Down"

QUESTION #99: Who played the kazoo on Ringo Starr's top-40 hit "You're Sixteen"?
A. Billy Preston
B. Paul McCartney
C. John Lennon
D. Harry Nilsson

QUESTION #100: John Lennon and Paul McCartney sang backing vocals on which Rolling Stones song?
A. "Tell Me"
B. "It's All Over Now"
C. "We Love You"
D. "Time Is On My Side"

QUESTION #101: What was the only U.S. top-40 hit that was credited on the label to "Paul & Linda McCartney"?
A. "Hi, Hi, Hi"
B. "Another Day"
C. "Live And Let Die"
D. "Uncle Albert / Admiral Halsey"

QUESTION #102: Approximately how many times did the Beatles perform at the Cavern Club?
A. 42
B. 92
C. 192
D. 292

QUESTION #103: After Pete Best was fired from the Beatles, he joined what other group?
A. Rory Storm & The Hurricanes
B. The Merseybeats
C. The Big Three
D. Lee Curtis & The All Stars

ANSWER #99: B. Paul McCartney
ANSWER #100: C. "We Love You"
ANSWER #101: D. "Uncle Albert / Admiral Halsey"
ANSWER #102: D. 292
ANSWER #103: D. Lee Curtis & The All Stars

QUESTION #104: Which instrument company gave George Harrison his first 12-string guitar?
A. Fender
B. Rickenbacker
C. Martin
D. Gibson

QUESTION #105: George Harrison wore his Sgt. Pepper uniform in which of his music videos?
A. "Got My Mind Set On You"
B. "When We Was Fab"
C. "All Those Years Ago"
D. "Blow Away"

QUESTION #106: Using the name Apollo C. Vermouth, which Beatle produced the 1968 British top-10 hit, "I'm The Urban Spaceman"?
A. John Lennon
B. Paul McCartney
C. George Harrison
D. Ringo Starr

QUESTION #107: Who directed the movie, "A Hard Day's Night"?
A. Paul McCartney
B. Richard Lester
C. Brian Epstein
D. George Martin

QUESTION #108: On the cover of the album "Abbey Road," which Beatle is walking in front of the others?
A. John Lennon
B. Paul McCartney
C. George Harrison
D. Ringo Starr

ANSWER #104: B. Rickenbacker
ANSWER #105: B. "When We Was Fab"
ANSWER #106: B. Paul McCartney. The song was a hit for the Bonzo Dog Doo-Dah Band.
ANSWER #107: B. Richard Lester
ANSWER #108: A. John Lennon

QUESTION #109: After the Beatles disbanded, who was the first member of the group to score a number-one solo hit in the U.S.?
A. John Lennon
B. Paul McCartney
C. George Harrison
D. Ringo Starr

QUESTION #110: Yoko Ono sang one line in which of these Beatles songs?
A. "Baby, You're A Rich Man"
B. "The Continuing Story Of Bungalow Bill"
C. "Yellow Submarine"
D. "The Ballad Of John And Yoko"

QUESTION #111: When the Beatles signed a management contract in 1962, they gave Brian Epstein what percentage of the group's earnings?
A. 10
B. 15
C. 20
D. 25

QUESTION #112: The film "Backbeat" followed the Beatles during their stay in which city?
A. Paris
B. Liverpool
C. Hamburg
D. New York

QUESTION #113: Which Beatle has daughters named Stella and Mary?
A. John Lennon
B. Paul McCartney
C. George Harrison
D. Ringo Starr

ANSWER #109: C. George Harrison
ANSWER #110: B. "The Continuing Story Of Bungalow Bill"
ANSWER #111: D. 25
ANSWER #112: C. Hamburg
ANSWER #113: B. Paul McCartney

QUESTION #114: What was the original title of the Beatles film, "Let It Be"?
A. "The End"
B. "The Long And Winding Road"
C. "Back In The USSR"
D. "Get Back"

❖ ❖ ❖

QUESTION #115: Which Beatle autograph is worth the least in the collector's market?
A. John Lennon
B. Paul McCartney
C. George Harrison
D. Ringo Starr

❖ ❖ ❖

QUESTION #116: Who designed the Beatles logo?
A. Brian Epstein
B. Eddie Stokes
C. Astrid Kirchherr
D. Peter Rogers

❖ ❖ ❖

QUESTION #117: What was the name of the first nightclub in Hamburg where the Beatles performed?
A. The Kino Club
B. The Jacaranda
C. The Indra
D. The Kaiserkeller

❖ ❖ ❖

QUESTION #118: Which "fifth Beatle" is pictured on the front cover of the album, "Sgt. Pepper's Lonely Hearts Club Band"?
A. George Martin
B. Billy Preston
C. Stuart Sutcliffe
D. Pete Best

ANSWER #114: D. "Get Back"
ANSWER #115: D. Ringo Starr
ANSWER #116: B. Eddie Stokes
ANSWER #117: C. The Indra
ANSWER #118: C. Stuart Sutcliffe

QUESTION #119: What unusual instrument is heard throughout the Beatles song, "Baby, You're A Rich Man"?
A. Electric violin
B. Clavioline
C. Xylophone
D. Dulcimer

QUESTION #120: Upon joining the Beatles, Ringo Starr was forced to cut his hair and do what else?
A. Fix his teeth
B. Stop smoking
C. Shave his beard
D. Lose 25 pounds

QUESTION #121: Who was the final Beatle to score a solo top-40 hit in the U.S.?
A. John Lennon
B. Paul McCartney
C. George Harrison
D. Ringo Starr

QUESTION #122: Which Wings song did Paul McCartney re-record for the soundtrack of his 1984 film, "Give My Regards To Broad Street"?
A. "Jet"
B. "Silly Love Songs"
C. "Helen Wheels"
D. "Let 'Em In"

QUESTION #123: The 1982 top-40 single "The Beatles Movie Medley" featured several snippets of Beatles hits, beginning with which song?
A. "All You Need Is Love"
B. "Get Back"
C. "Magical Mystery Tour"
D. "A Hard Day's Night"

ANSWER #119: B. Clavioline
ANSWER #120: C. Shave his beard
ANSWER #121: B. Paul McCartney
ANSWER #122: B. "Silly Love Songs"
ANSWER #123: C. "Magical Mystery Tour"

QUESTION #124: A Beatles cartoon show aired from 1965 to 1969 on which U.S. television network?
A. ABC
B. CBS
C. NBC
D. PBS

❖ ❖ ❖

QUESTION #125: On the first season of the Beatles cartoon series, the opening theme began with a riff from which of the group's songs?
A. "She Love's You"
B. "Twist And Shout"
C. "I Feel Fine"
D. "A Hard Day's Night"

❖ ❖ ❖

QUESTION #126: In 1964, John Lennon was offended when the press began comparing the Beatles to which comedy team?
A. The Three Stooges
B. The Marx Brothers
C. Abbott and Costello
D. Laurel and Hardy

❖ ❖ ❖

QUESTION #127: What was the original title of the song, "Hey Bulldog"?
A. "Hey Bullman"
B. "Hey Bullgrog"
C. "Hey Bullhog"
D. "Hey Bullfrog"

❖ ❖ ❖

QUESTION #128: The title of which of these Beatles songs is NOT mentioned in the lyrics?
A. "I Am The Walrus"
B. "For You Blue"
C. "Thank You Girl"
D. "A Day In The Life"

ANSWER #124: A. ABC
ANSWER #125: D. "A Hard Day's Night"
ANSWER #126: B. The Marx Brothers
ANSWER #127: D. "Hey Bullfrog"
ANSWER #128: D. "A Day In The Life"

QUESTION #129: Several words in the lyrics of "Across The Universe" are sung in which language?
A. Cherokee
B. French
C. Yiddish
D. Sanskrit

QUESTION #130: Brian Epstein had little success when he managed which British Invasion group in 1966?
A. The Kinks
B. The Who
C. The Moody Blues
D. Herman's Hermits

QUESTION #131: George Harrison and Eric Clapton co-wrote which hit for the group, Cream?
A. "Crossroads"
B. "White Room"
C. "Badge"
D. "Sunshine Of Your Love"

QUESTION #132: Mick Jagger provided backing vocals on which of these Beatles songs?
A. "Birthday"
B. "Hey Jude"
C. "Day Tripper"
D. "Baby, You're A Rich Man"

QUESTION #133: Which Beatle hosted his own syndicated radio show in the early-1980s?
A. John Lennon
B. Paul McCartney
C. George Harrison
D. Ringo Starr

ANSWER #129: D. Sanskrit
ANSWER #130: C. The Moody Blues
ANSWER #131: C. "Badge"
ANSWER #132: D. "Baby, You're A Rich Man"
ANSWER #133: D. Ringo Starr hosted a program called "Ringo's Yellow Submarine."

QUESTION #134: Which Beatle made a cameo appearance in the 1977 spoof film, "The Rutles"?
A. John Lennon
B. Paul McCartney
C. George Harrison
D. Ringo Starr

QUESTION #135: Who was the first non-Beatle to record and release a Lennon-McCartney song?
A. Helen Shapiro
B. Del Shannon
C. Tony Sheridan
D. Kenny Lynch

QUESTION #136: In 1980, how many days did Paul McCartney spend in a Tokyo jail cell?
A. 1
B. 5
C. 10
D. 15

QUESTION #137: Which member of the Beatles organization can be heard at the start of the song, "Revolution 9"?
A. Dick James
B. Allen Klein
C. Alistair Taylor
D. Brian Epstein

QUESTION #138: When the Beatles traveled to Greece in 1967, they were there to do what?
A. Buy an island
B. Buy a pig farm
C. Buy some guitars
D. Find a wife for Ringo

ANSWER #134: C. George Harrison
ANSWER #135: D. Kenny Lynch recorded "Misery" after the song was rejected by Helen Shapiro.
ANSWER #136: C. 10
ANSWER #137: C. Alistair Taylor
ANSWER #138: A. Buy an island, but they changed their minds after traveling along the coast.

QUESTION #139: Which of these Paul McCartney hits was NOT written for a movie?
A. "Live And Let Die"
B. "Spies Like Us"
C. "Coming Up"
D. "No More Lonely Nights"

❖ ❖ ❖

QUESTION #140: What small but important role did Raymond Jones play in the history of the Beatles?
A. He gave John Lennon a harmonica
B. He lent Paul McCartney his first guitar
C. He requested a Beatles record at NEMS
D. He booked the Beatles at the Cavern Club

❖ ❖ ❖

QUESTION #141: Which Beatles song featured only one instrument, an acoustic guitar?
A. "And I Love Her"
B. "If I Fell"
C. "Blackbird"
D. "There's A Place"

❖ ❖ ❖

QUESTION #142: Which blues singer is mentioned in the lyrics of the Beatles song, "For You Blue"?
A. Robert Johnson
B. Albert King
C. Elmore James
D. Big Joe Turner

❖ ❖ ❖

QUESTION #143: Which Beatles album was given a poor review by *Rolling Stone* magazine?
A. "Let It Be"
B. "Magical Mystery Tour"
C. "Abbey Road"
D. "Rubber Soul"

ANSWER #139: C. "Coming Up"
ANSWER #140: C. He requested a Beatles record at NEMS from Brian Epstein who was working at the counter.
ANSWER #141: C. "Blackbird"
ANSWER #142: C. Elmore James
ANSWER #143: A. "Let It Be"

QUESTION #144: The Beatles were in the middle of a three-week concert stint in which city when they learned about their first number-one single in the U.S.?
A. Hamburg
B. Liverpool
C. London
D. Paris

❖ ❖ ❖

QUESTION #145: The single version of which Beatles song is longer than the album version?
A. "Get Back"
B. "We Can Work It Out"
C. "Day Tripper"
D. "Paperback Writer"

❖ ❖ ❖

QUESTION #146: The song "Dear Prudence" was written about the sister of which actress?
A. Lynn Redgrave
B. Bridget Bardot
C. Sophia Loren
D. Mia Farrow

❖ ❖ ❖

QUESTION #147: In 1963, which Beatle had a column in the British newspaper, "The Daily Express"?
A. John Lennon
B. Paul McCartney
C. George Harrison
D. Ringo Starr

❖ ❖ ❖

QUESTION #148: In 2003, which Beatle starred in an Emmy Award-winning television special on the A&E network?
A. John Lennon
B. Paul McCartney
C. George Harrison
D. Ringo Starr

ANSWER #144: D. Paris
ANSWER #145: A. "Get Back"
ANSWER #146: D. Mia Farrow
ANSWER #147: C. George Harrison
ANSWER #148: B. Paul McCartney

QUESTION #149: Which Beatles song begins with Paul McCartney counting to four?
A. "Helter Skelter"
B. "Twist And Shout"
C. "I Saw Her Standing There"
D. "Get Back"

❖ ❖ ❖

QUESTION #150: What year did the original Cavern Club close?
A. 1963
B. 1968
C. 1973
D. 1978

❖ ❖ ❖

QUESTION #151: John Lennon wrote "I Call Your Name" for which other artist, who used the song as a B-side on a single?
A. Cilla Black
B. Billy J. Kramer
C. Peter & Gordon
D. Herman's Hermits

❖ ❖ ❖

QUESTION #152: Paul McCartney co-wrote which of his 1980s hits with Elvis Costello?
A. "Take It Away"
B. "Spies Like Us"
C. "Coming Up"
D. "My Brave Face"

❖ ❖ ❖

QUESTION #153: In October 1962, the Beatles made their first-ever television appearance on which British program?
A. "Tuesday Rendezvous"
B. "Discs A Gogo"
C. "People And Places"
D. "Roundup"

ANSWER #149: C. "I Saw Her Standing There"
ANSWER #150: C. 1973
ANSWER #151: B. Billy J. Kramer
ANSWER #152: D. "My Brave Face"
ANSWER #153: C. "People And Places"

QUESTION #154: Who was the first Beatle to perform in the former Soviet Union?
A. John Lennon
B. Paul McCartney
C. George Harrison
D. Ringo Starr

❖ ❖ ❖

QUESTION #155: When did John Lennon record the demo version of "Free As A Bird"?
A. 1957
B. 1967
C. 1977
D. 1980

❖ ❖ ❖

QUESTION #156: Which Beatle performed on the all-star protest song, "Sun City"?
A. John Lennon
B. Paul McCartney
C. George Harrison
D. Ringo Starr

❖ ❖ ❖

QUESTION #157: The television film "Ringo," which starred Ringo Starr, Art Carney and Vincent Price, was broadcast in what year?
A. 1968
B. 1978
C. 1988
D. 1998

❖ ❖ ❖

QUESTION #158: Which Buddy Holly classic was the first song John Lennon learned how to play on the guitar?
A. "Peggy Sue"
B. "That'll Be The Day"
C. "Not Fade Away"
D. "Rave On"

ANSWER #154: B. Paul McCartney
ANSWER #155: C. 1977
ANSWER #156: D. Ringo Starr
ANSWER #157: B. 1978
ANSWER #158: B. "That'll Be The Day"

QUESTION #159: A remake of which Beatles song earned a Grammy award in the 1970s?

A. "Got To Get You Into My Life"
B. "If You Won't See Me"
C. "Come Together"
D. "Helter Skelter"

QUESTION #160: When the New York Times accused the Beatles of musically "ripping off" other artists, which Beatle sent the writer of the article an angry letter?

A. John Lennon
B. Paul McCartney
C. George Harrison
D. Ringo Starr

QUESTION #161: During his early years with the Beatles, George Harrison primarily used which brand of guitar?

A. Gretsch
B. Fender
C. Gibson
D. Epiphone

QUESTION #162: John Lennon's "Lost Weekend" separation from Yoko Ono lasted how long?

A. 3 months
B. 6 months
C. 12 months
D. 18 months

ANSWER #159: A. "Got To Get You Into My Life" by Earth, Wind & Fire won a Grammy Award in 1977.
ANSWER #160: A. John Lennon
ANSWER #161: A. Gretsch
ANSWER #162: D. 18 months

QUESTION #163: A doll on the cover of "Sgt. Pepper's Lonely Hearts Club Band" is wearing a sweater that features the name of which rock group?
A. The Cricketts
B. The Hollies
C. The Rolling Stones
D. The Ventures

QUESTION #164: Which of these chart-topping Beatles singles was never issued in stereo?
A. "I Want To Hold Your Hand"
B. "She Loves You"
C. "Can't Buy Me Love"
D. "Love Me Do"

QUESTION #165: Who bought John Lennon's last English home when John and Yoko moved to New York City?
A. George Martin
B. Paul McCartney
C. George Harrison
D. Ringo Starr

QUESTION #166: Who was the first Beatle to release a solo album?
A. John Lennon
B. Paul McCartney
C. George Harrison
D. Ringo Starr

QUESTION #167: The final chord of "A Day In The Life" lasts how many seconds?
A. 35
B. 45
C. 55
D. 65

ANSWER #163: C. The Rolling Stones
ANSWER #164: B. "She Loves You"
ANSWER #165: D. Ringo Starr
ANSWER #166: C. George Harrison
ANSWER #167: B. 45 seconds

QUESTION #168: What was the only new song on Paul McCartney's 1984 album, "Give My Regards To Broad Street"?
A. "Ebony And Ivory"
B. "Coming Up"
C. "No More Lonely Nights"
D. "Take It Away"

QUESTION #169: Which opening act for the Beatles quit a 1964 U.S. tour because their performances were constantly drowned out by screaming Beatles fans?
A. The Bill Black Combo
B. Jackie DeShannon
C. The Exciters
D. The Righteous Brothers

QUESTION #170: Which early Beatles track was co-written by Burt Bacharach?
A. "Anna (Go To Him)"
B. "Baby It's You"
C. "A Taste Of Honey"
D. "Chains"

QUESTION #171: Which Beatles album spent the most number of weeks on the U.S. album charts?
A. "Revolver"
B. "The White Album"
C. "Abbey Road"
D. "Sgt. Pepper's Lonely Hearts Club Band"

QUESTION #172: Which Beatle had a tattoo on both arms?
A. John Lennon
B. Paul McCartney
C. George Harrison
D. Ringo Starr

ANSWER #168: C. "No More Lonely Nights"
ANSWER #169: D. The Righteous Brothers
ANSWER #170: B. "Baby It's You"
ANSWER #171: D. "Sgt. Pepper's Lonely Hearts Club Band"
ANSWER #172: D. Ringo Starr

QUESTION #173: Which Beatle had the unofficial duty to make sure the band's instruments were tuned correctly?
A. John Lennon
B. Paul McCartney
C. George Harrison
D. Ringo Starr

QUESTION #174: What was the first Beatles single to hit the top-40 in the U.S.?
A. "I Saw Her Standing There"
B. "I Want To Hold Your Hand"
C. "She Loves You"
D. "Please Please Me"

QUESTION #175: Which Beatle met his future wife on the set of the film, "A Hard Day's Night"?
A. John Lennon
B. Paul McCartney
C. George Harrison
D. Ringo Starr

QUESTION #176: Who played the drums on the Beatles songs, "Love Me Do" and "P.S. I Love You"?
A. Ringo Starr
B. Andy White
C. Pete Best
D. Paul McCartney

ANSWER #173: C. George Harrison
ANSWER #174: B. "I Want To Hold Your Hand" hit the charts in January 1964.
ANSWER #175: C. George Harrison met Pattie Boyd, who was one of the schoolgirls on the train.
ANSWER #176: B. Andy White played the drums on these two tracks at the insistence of producer George Martin.

QUESTION #177: Which Beatles song was originally written for the 1957 Broadway musical, "The Music Man"?
A. "Matchbox"
B. "Anna (Go To Him)"
C. "Honey Don't"
D. "Till There Was You"

QUESTION #178: Which Beatle was the executive producer of the Madonna film, "Shanghai Surprise"?
A. John Lennon
B. Paul McCartney
C. George Harrison
D. Ringo Starr

QUESTION #179: In 2001, the city of Liverpool renamed its airport after which Beatle?
A. John Lennon
B. Paul McCartney
C. George Harrison
D. Ringo Starr

QUESTION #180: Which Olympic athlete was pictured on the cover of the album, "Sgt. Pepper's Lonely Hearts Club Band"?
A. Jim Thorpe
B. Johnny Weissmuller
C. Jesse Owens
D. Cathy Rigby

QUESTION #181: Which of these Beatles songs did Paul McCartney write about his future wife, Linda?
A. "And I Love Her"
B. "Hello Little Girl"
C. "Two Of Us"
D. "I Call Your Name"

ANSWER #177: D. "Till There Was You"
ANSWER #178: C. George Harrison
ANSWER #179: A. John Lennon
ANSWER #180: B. Johnny Weissmuller
ANSWER #181: C. "Two Of Us"

QUESTION #182: George Harrison claimed that which of his solo hits did not have a melody?
A. "My Sweet Lord"
B. "What Is Life"
C. "All Those Years Ago"
D. "Dark Horse"

QUESTION #183: Which Beatles song was played for the astronauts on the final NASA Space Shuttle mission?
A. "The Long And Winding Road"
B. "Get Back"
C. "Yellow Submarine"
D. "Good Day Sunshine"

QUESTION #184: In 1969, disc jockeys in which city began publicizing the "Paul is dead" rumor?
A. Chicago
B. Cleveland
C. Detroit
D. Buffalo

QUESTION #185: After the Beatles disbanded, which of these artists was NOT produced by George Martin?
A. Kenny Rogers
B. Neil Sedaka
C. Cheap Trick
D. REO Speedwagon

QUESTION #186: Which member of Pink Floyd worked with Paul McCartney on his 1999 solo album, "Run Devil Run"?
A. Roger Waters
B. David Gilmour
C. Nick Mason
D. Richard Wright

ANSWER #182: A. "My Sweet Lord"
ANSWER #183: D. "Good Day Sunshine"
ANSWER #184: C. Detroit
ANSWER #185: D. REO Speedwagon
ANSWER #186: B. David Gilmour

QUESTION #187: As a member of the Traveling Wilburys, George Harrison was known as Nelson Wilbury as well as what other name?
A. Spike Wilbury
B. Clayton Wilbury
C. Boo Wilbury
D. Muddy Wilbury

QUESTION #188: Who came up with the idea to add a string quartet on the song, "Yesterday"?
A. John Lennon
B. Paul McCartney
C. Brian Epstein
D. George Martin

QUESTION #189: After drummer Denny Seiwell quit the group Wings, Paul McCartney was forced to play the drums on which album?
A. "Band On The Run"
B. "Wings Over America"
C. "Venus And Mars"
D. "Ram"

QUESTION #190: In 1965, the father of which Beatle recorded the single, "That's My Life (My Love And My Home)"?
A. John Lennon
B. Paul McCartney
C. George Harrison
D. Ringo Starr

QUESTION #191: What was the first Beatles song to feature backward tape loops?
A. "Got To Get You Into My Life"
B. "Strawberry Fields Forever"
C. "Taxman"
D. "Rain"

ANSWER #187: A. Spike Wilbury
ANSWER #188: D. George Martin
ANSWER #189: A. "Band On The Run"
ANSWER #190: A. John Lennon. His father, Alfred Lennon, released the single as by Freddie Lennon.
ANSWER #191: D. "Rain"

QUESTION #192: The Mike Sammes Singers provided backing vocals on which Beatles song?
A. "All You Need Is Love"
B. "I Am The Walrus"
C. "Yellow Submarine"
D. "Hey Jude"

❖ ❖ ❖

QUESTION #193: In 1995, which Beatle appeared in a television commercial for Pizza Hut?
A. John Lennon
B. Paul McCartney
C. George Harrison
D. Ringo Starr

❖ ❖ ❖

QUESTION #194: Which Beatle organized the charity project, the Concerts for the People of Kampuchea?
A. John Lennon
B. Paul McCartney
C. George Harrison
D. Ringo Starr

❖ ❖ ❖

QUESTION #195: George Harrison launched his last-ever tour in 1991 when he joined Eric Clapton for a series of concerts in what country?
A. Japan
B. England
C. Germany
D. Canada

❖ ❖ ❖

QUESTION #196: Which Beatle played all of the instruments on his debut solo album?
A. John Lennon
B. Paul McCartney
C. George Harrison
D. Ringo Starr

ANSWER #192: B. "I Am The Walrus"
ANSWER #193: D. Ringo Starr
ANSWER #194: B. Paul McCartney
ANSWER #195: A. Japan
ANSWER #196: B. Paul McCartney

QUESTION #197: Who wrote Ringo Starr's 1981 hit, "Wrack My Brain"?
A. John Lennon
B. Paul McCartney
C. George Harrison
D. Harry Nilsson

❖ ❖ ❖

QUESTION #198: In 1975, which Beatle released a greatest-hits compilation album that was titled, "Blast From Your Past"?
A. John Lennon
B. Paul McCartney
C. George Harrison
D. Ringo Starr

❖ ❖ ❖

QUESTION #199: Which Beatle used a self-portrait on the cover of a solo album?
A. John Lennon
B. Paul McCartney
C. George Harrison
D. Ringo Starr

❖ ❖ ❖

QUESTION #200: Which album did the Rolling Stones record in response to the Beatles, "Sgt. Pepper's Lonely Hearts Club Band"?
A. "Their Satanic Majesties Request"
B. "Between The Buttons"
C. "Beggars Banquet"
D. "Aftermath"

❖ ❖ ❖

QUESTION #201: One of the first releases on Apple Records, "Sour Milk Sea" by Jackie Lomax was written and produced by which Beatle?
A. John Lennon
B. Paul McCartney
C. George Harrison
D. Ringo Starr

ANSWER #197: C. George Harrison
ANSWER #198: D. Ringo Starr
ANSWER #199: A. John Lennon
ANSWER #200: A. "Their Satanic Majesties Request"
ANSWER #201: C. George Harrison

QUESTION #202: Before he worked with the Beatles, George Martin released his own single under what name?
A. George M. Washington
B. Skiffle Samuels
C. Ray Cathode
D. Martin N. Lewis

❖ ❖ ❖

QUESTION #203: Although "Magical Mystery Tour" was issued as a 12-inch LP in the U.S., how was the soundtrack originally issued in Britain?
A. A booklet of five 45s
B. A two EP set
C. A three EP set
D. A double LP

❖ ❖ ❖

QUESTION #204: Which song was missing from the original British release of the Paul McCartney & Wings album, "Band On The Run"?
A. "Helen Wheels"
B. "Jet"
C. "Band On The Run"
D. "Nineteen Hundred And Eighty-Five"

❖ ❖ ❖

QUESTION #205: When the Beatles signed with EMI-Parlophone Records, the contract period was for how many years, maximum?
A. 5 years
B. 8 years
C. 12 years
D. 15 years

ANSWER #202: C. Ray Cathode
ANSWER #203: B. A two EP set
ANSWER #204: A. "Helen Wheels"
ANSWER #205: A. 5 years

QUESTION #206: "Lucy In The Sky With Diamonds" was inspired by a drawing Julian Lennon painted of his friend, Lucy. What was Lucy's last name?

A. O'Richards
B. O'Lucas
C. O'Donnell
D. O'Henry

❖ ❖ ❖

QUESTION #207: Who is the only Beatle wearing blue jeans on the cover of "Abbey Road"?

A. John Lennon
B. Paul McCartney
C. George Harrison
D. Ringo Starr

❖ ❖ ❖

QUESTION #208: Shortly after the Beatles signed a recording contract with EMI-Parlophone, which Beatle began taking piano lessons?

A. John Lennon
B. Paul McCartney
C. George Harrison
D. Ringo Starr

❖ ❖ ❖

QUESTION #209: In what year did Paul and Linda McCartney perform on "Saturday Night Live"?

A. 1975
B. 1980
C. 1985
D. 1990

ANSWER #206: C. O'Donnell
ANSWER #207: C. George Harrison
ANSWER #208: B. Paul McCartney
ANSWER #209: B. 1980

QUESTION #210: In 1970, Elvis Presley's backing vocal group the Jordanaires provided vocals on a solo album by which Beatle?
A. John Lennon
B. Paul McCartney
C. George Harrison
D. Ringo Starr

QUESTION #211: What is the best-selling Beatles single in the U.S.?
A. "A Hard Day's Night"
B. "Hey Jude"
C. "Let It Be"
D. "I Want To Hold Your Hand"

QUESTION #212: For a short time, which Beatle was the brother-in-law of Mick Fleetwood of the group Fleetwood Mac?
A. John Lennon
B. Paul McCartney
C. George Harrison
D. Ringo Starr

QUESTION #213: "Two Of Us," a fictional film about Lennon and McCartney, aired on which U.S. television network?
A. ABC
B. VH-1
C. HBO
D. NBC

QUESTION #214: Which Paul McCartney album included two duets with Michael Jackson?
A. "McCartney II"
B. "Tug Of War"
C. "Pipes Of Peace"
D. "Give My Regards To Broad Street"

ANSWER #210: D. Ringo Starr
ANSWER #211: D. "I Want To Hold Your Hand"
ANSWER #212: C. George Harrison
ANSWER #213: B. VH-1
ANSWER #214: C. "Pipes Of Peace"

QUESTION #215: Which Beatle co-founded a label called Pumkinhead Records?
A. John Lennon
B. Paul McCartney
C. George Harrison
D. Ringo Starr

QUESTION #216: Four songs on which John Lennon album featured the musical backing of Frank Zappa and the Mothers of Invention?
A. "Milk And Honey"
B. "Mind Games"
C. "Imagine"
D. "Some Time In New York City"

QUESTION #217: Which Beatle has appeared on the cover of *Rolling Stone* magazine the most number of times?
A. John Lennon
B. Paul McCartney
C. George Harrison
D. Ringo Starr

QUESTION #218: Which Beatles song was originally recorded by the Top Notes?
A. "Ain't She Sweet"
B. "Money"
C. "Twist And Shout"
D. "Anna (Go To Him)"

QUESTION #219: Which of these Beatles songs was a British top-10 hit for three different artists?
A. "Hey Jude"
B. "With A Little Help From My Friends"
C. "Yesterday"
D. "Lady Madonna"

ANSWER #215: D. Ringo Starr
ANSWER #216: D. Some Time In New York City
ANSWER #217: A. John Lennon
ANSWER #218: C. "Twist And Shout" was later recorded by the Isley Brothers.
ANSWER #219: B. "With A Little Help From My Friends"

QUESTION #220: At the 1975 Grammy Awards, which Beatle was a guest presenter for the Record of the Year award?
A. John Lennon
B. Paul McCartney
C. George Harrison
D. Ringo Starr

QUESTION #221: When Paul McCartney secretly began recording his first solo album, he hid his identity by booking studio time under what name?
A. Billy Shears
B. Billy Barton
C. Billy Martin
D. Billy Bradshaw

QUESTION #222: John Lennon's son Julian sang which Beatles song in a commercial for Allstate Insurance?
A. "Eight Days A Week"
B. "Drive My Car"
C. "When I'm 64"
D. "She's Leaving Home"

QUESTION #223: Which song on the Beatles debut album did the group decide to record at the last minute?
A. "Misery"
B. "Anna (Go To Him)"
C. "Chains"
D. "Twist And Shout"

QUESTION #224: Who made the following statement about the Beatles... "Oh, I never liked them anyway – their music is horrible!"
A. Ed Sullivan
B. Imelda Marcos
C. Frank Sinatra
D. Elvis Presley

ANSWER #220: A. John Lennon
ANSWER #221: C. Billy Martin
ANSWER #222: C. "When I'm 64"
ANSWER #223: D. "Twist And Shout"
ANSWER #224: B. Imelda Marcos

QUESTION #225: How much did Michael Jackson pay to buy the publishing rights of nearly all the Beatles songs written by Lennon and McCartney?
A. $4.75 million
B. $47.5 million
C. $97.5 million
D. $197.5 million

QUESTION #226: Which Beatles song did Paul McCartney claim was a parody of the Beach Boys sound?
A. "Ob-La-Di, Ob-La-Da"
B. "She's A Woman"
C. "I Want To Hold Your Hand"
D. "Back In The U.S.S.R."

QUESTION #227: After completing the sessions for the album "Rock 'N' Roll," John Lennon was unable to retrieve the master tapes from producer Phil Spector for what reason?
A. Spector threatened Lennon with a gun.
B. Spector was in a serious auto accident.
C. Lennon owed Spector a large fee.
D. Spector had misplaced the tapes.

QUESTION #228: When the Beatles performed at Carnegie Hall in 1964, what was the price of the most expensive ticket?
A. $5.50
B. $15.50
C. $25.50
D. $35.50

QUESTION #229: Which Beatle won the most number of Grammy Awards during the 1970s?
A. John Lennon
B. Paul McCartney
C. George Harrison
D. Ringo Starr

ANSWER #225: B. $47.5 million
ANSWER #226: D. "Back In The U.S.S.R."
ANSWER #227: B. Spector was in a serious auto accident.
ANSWER #228: A. $5.50
ANSWER #229: B. Paul McCartney earned three Grammys.

QUESTION #230: Billy Preston recorded which Beatles song for the B-side of his top-40 hit, "Will It Go Round In Circles"?
A. "Blackbird"
B. "Yesterday"
C. "Let It Be"
D. "Don't Let Me Down"

❖ ❖ ❖

QUESTION #231: Who was the best man at John and Yoko's wedding?
A. Brian Epstein
B. Peter Brown
C. George Martin
D. Paul McCartney

❖ ❖ ❖

QUESTION #232: Who was the best man at John and Cynthia Powell's wedding?
A. Brian Epstein
B. Peter Brown
C. George Martin
D. Paul McCartney

❖ ❖ ❖

QUESTION #233: Which Beatle used the most number of pseudonyms on album credits, including Reverend Fred Ghurkin, Mel Torment and Fred Zimmerman?
A. John Lennon
B. Paul McCartney
C. George Harrison
D. Ringo Starr

❖ ❖ ❖

QUESTION #234: The Beatles first began printing the lyrics of their songs on the cover of which album?
A. "Rubber Soul"
B. "Let It Be"
C. "Revolver"
D. "Sgt. Pepper's Lonely Hearts Club Band"

ANSWER #230: A. "Blackbird"
ANSWER #231: B. Peter Brown
ANSWER #232: A. Brian Epstein
ANSWER #233: A. John Lennon
ANSWER #234: D. "Sgt. Pepper's Lonely Hearts Club Band"

QUESTION #235: In 1987, Paul McCartney recorded the solo album "Choba B CCCP," which was released only where?
A. India
B. Japan
C. The Soviet Union
D. Switzerland

QUESTION #236: In 1975, which Beatle spent three hours as the guest deejay on the Scott Muni program on WNEW-FM in New York City?
A. John Lennon
B. Paul McCartney
C. George Harrison
D. Ringo Starr

QUESTION #237: In January 1968, which Beatle traveled to India in order to record at the EMI studio in Bombay?
A. John Lennon
B. Paul McCartney
C. George Harrison
D. Ringo Starr

QUESTION #238: Which of these Beatles singles did not reach #1 on the U.S. charts?
A. "Let It Be"
B. "Lady Madonna"
C. "Eight Days A Week"
D. "Yesterday"

QUESTION #239: In what year did Ringo Starr team with Buck Owens to record a duet of "Act Naturally"?
A. 1969
B. 1979
C. 1989
D. 1999

ANSWER #235: C. The Soviet Union
ANSWER #236: A. John Lennon
ANSWER #237: C. George Harrison
ANSWER #238: B. "Lady Madonna"
ANSWER #239: C. 1989

QUESTION #240: The Beatles won an Academy Award in the "Best Original Song Score" category for which film?
A. "Magical Mystery Tour"
B. "Yellow Submarine"
C. "Help!"
D. "Let It Be"

❖ ❖ ❖

QUESTION #241: Which musician introduced George Harrison to traditional Indian music?
A. Steve Winwood
B. Jeff Beck
C. Eric Clapton
D. David Crosby

❖ ❖ ❖

QUESTION #242: Two years before the Beatles first charted in the U.S., who was the first British rock act to top the U.S. charts?
A. The Tornados
B. Cliff Richard
C. The Springfields
D. The Rolling Stones

❖ ❖ ❖

QUESTION #243: During their early trips to the U.S., the Beatles were ordered by Brian Epstein to avoid discussing what with the media?
A. Elvis Presley
B. Politics
C. Marriage
D. Sports

❖ ❖ ❖

QUESTION #244: Who did John Lennon hire as the guitarist in the Plastic Ono Band for the concert and film, "Live Peace In Toronto 1969"?
A. Rory Gallagher
B. Robby Krieger
C. Eric Clapton
D. Steve Cropper

ANSWER #240: D. "Let It Be"
ANSWER #241: D. David Crosby
ANSWER #242: A. The Tornados
ANSWER #243: B. Politics
ANSWER #244: C. Eric Clapton

QUESTION #245: After the Beatles, who was the next British Invasion artist to top the U.S. singles charts?
A. The Animals
B. The Rolling Stones
C. Herman's Hermits
D. Peter & Gordon

QUESTION #246: The cover of the "Sgt. Pepper" album featured a small television owned by which Beatle?
A. John Lennon
B. Paul McCartney
C. George Harrison
D. Ringo Starr

QUESTION #247: Magic Alex was a friend of the Beatles and the head of the group's business venture, Apple Electronics. What was Magic Alex's last name?
A. Martha
B. Mardonis
C. Margolis
D. Mardas

QUESTION #248: In what year did Ringo Starr begin his multi-artist "All-Starr Band" tours?
A. 1989
B. 1994
C. 1999
D. 2004

QUESTION #249: What is the only Beatles song to feature John Lennon on bass guitar?
A. "Let It Be"
B. "Hey Jude"
C. "Birthday"
D. "The Long And Winding Road"

ANSWER #245: D. Peter & Gordon
ANSWER #246: B. Paul McCartney. The Sony brand television is now exhibited at a museum in Japan.
ANSWER #247: D. Mardas
ANSWER #248: A. 1989
ANSWER #249: D. "The Long And Winding Road"

QUESTION #250: Due to legal reasons, which Beatle was forced to use the pseudonym, L'Angelo Misterioso, when he co-wrote a song in 1969?

A. John Lennon
B. Paul McCartney
C. George Harrison
D. Ringo Starr

ANSWER #250: C. George Harrison

Other Books By Steven Miller:

Tom Petty Trivia Book

Beatles Trivia Book, Volume 1

Beatles Trivia Book, Volume 2

Beatles Trivia Book, Volume 3

Please email us with any questions or comments at
westernreserve@mail.com. Also, please email us if you find any of
these trivia questions posted on another site or platform.

Printed in Great Britain
by Amazon